Earth ALERT

CONTENTS

By Roger Cook

earth ALERT

PREDICT

What do you think this
book could be about?

With the population of the world at more
than six and a half billion people, and
projected to grow by 80 million each year,
the impact of humanity on this planet and
its environment is immense.

For decades, scientists have been warning
about what would happen if we continue
to pump "greenhouse" gases into the
atmosphere, trapping heat from the sun
and raising the Earth's temperature.

Now, as we face unpredictable and extreme
weather phenomena, melting glaciers,
rising ocean levels, droughts, deforestation
and threatened or extinct animals species,
the evidence suggests that the scientists
have been right. Global warming is
happening, and people are **to blame**.

WORD ORIGIN

atmosphere
phenomena
Where are they from?

CLARIFY

projected
humanity
...unpredictable

... six and a half billion
people ...

sun

QUESTION

What kinds of
human activities
do you think
would contribute
to global
warming?

incoming energy from the sun

trapped heat

earth

The greenhouse effect – the
surface of the Earth absorbs solar
energy from the sun. The build-up of
greenhouse gases in the atmosphere
traps some of this heat, contributing
to global warming.

WORD ORIGIN

oxygen
temperature
Where are they from?

percentage

Nitrogen (78%)

Oxygen (21%)

Argon (0.9%)

Carbon dioxide and other gases (0.1%)

gases found in the atmosphere

The Greenhouse Effect

The Earth is wrapped in a blanket of air called the atmosphere. The atmosphere is mostly made up of nitrogen, oxygen and greenhouse gases, such as carbon dioxide, methane, nitrous oxide and water vapour.

All living things on this planet need oxygen and carbon dioxide to survive. People and animals inhale oxygen for energy and growth and exhale carbon dioxide. Trees and other plants take in this carbon dioxide, use it to make food and then release oxygen – the oxygen we breathe.

Carbon dioxide and other greenhouse gases also play a very important part in controlling the Earth's temperature. As energy from the sun passes through the atmosphere and reaches the Earth's surface, it is converted to heat, warming the land and water. Naturally occurring greenhouse gases act like a greenhouse, trapping this heat and preventing some of it from escaping back into space. This process is called the "natural greenhouse effect" and, without it, life on this planet would not be possible.

Over the past century, human activity has been increasing the levels of greenhouse gases in the atmosphere, upsetting the natural greenhouse effect. Scientists fear that this continued increase is causing the Earth to heat up even more, in an effect called "global warming".

Trees and other plants provide the planet with oxygen.

... all living things ... need oxygen ...

CLARIFY

inhale
exhale

How Global Warming is Caused

Scientists today believe that global warming is linked to human activities.

Air Pollution

The vast increase in greenhouse gases is linked to the world's constant demand for more energy and food and more land on which to produce it. The burning of fossil fuels releases carbon dioxide into the atmosphere. Fossil fuels, such as coal, oil and natural gas, are used to power electricity plants and factories, heat homes, run cars, trains, trucks and aeroplanes. Every time a fossil fuel is burnt, more carbon dioxide floats up into the atmosphere.

Rubbish sent to landfills produces a greenhouse gas called methane. Methane is also released from human and animal waste, swamps and rice fields.

In some poorer countries, man-made chemicals, such as chlorofluorocarbons, or CFCs, are used in aerosols, fridges and the making of foam plastics. Not only do they trap large amounts of heat in the atmosphere, they also destroy the ozone layer.

an aerial view showing diggers at a landfill site

OPINION

What is your opinion of global warming?

What types of countries do you think contribute most to the increase of greenhouse gases? Rich or poor countries? Why?

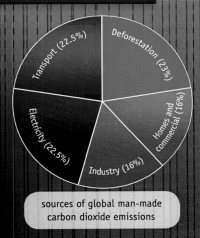

sources of global man-made carbon dioxide emissions

Transport (22.5%)
Deforestation (23%)
Homes and commercial (16%)
Industry (16%)
Electricity (22.5%)

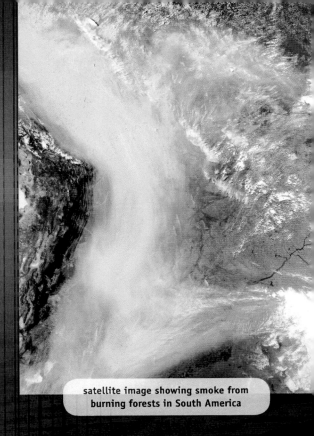

satellite image showing smoke from burning forests in South America

... more carbon dioxide floats up into the atmosphere ...

air pollution in China

INFERENCE

What can you infer about many people's attitudes towards the Earth?

The "slash and burn" technique destroys forests and sends more carbon dioxide into the atmosphere.

CLARIFY

photosynthesis
regulate
razed

trees killed by a combination of acid rain and other pollution

QUESTION

What do you think is meant by ...

Not only does it take away a potential sink to trap carbon dioxide ... ?

1975   1992   2000

These satellite images show the extent of deforestation in Bolivia in 1975, 1992 and 2000.

Deforestation

Forests, particularly rainforests, play a vital role on Earth and are often described as the "lungs of our planet". They absorb carbon dioxide from the atmosphere to use in photosynthesis. This helps to regulate the natural greenhouse effect, producing approximately 20 per cent of the world's oxygen. But the Earth is losing millions of hectares of forest every year. It is being razed for logging, cattle pasture, crops and mining, and for building highways and human settlements.

Scientists have discovered that deforestation – the cutting down, burning and damaging of forests – is a major cause of global warming. Not only does it take away a potential sink to trap carbon dioxide, it also pumps extra carbon dioxide into the atmosphere as people clear forests using the "slash and burn" technique. People are producing more carbon dioxide than the planet can handle, and there are fewer and fewer trees to absorb it.

Forests are also disappearing because of acid rain, which occurs when air pollutants from industrial processes and the burning of fossil fuels react with water in the Earth's atmosphere. This "acidic water" can get carried for hundreds of kilometres by the wind before it is released as acid rain. Acid rain damages and burns the leaves of trees and reduces their ability to absorb nutrients and withstand cold.

As the areas of deforestation grow larger and larger, the impact on the global climate grows. Scientists predict that, if the current rate of deforestation around the world continues, there will be no rainforests left by the year 2050.

SUMMARY CHART

How Global Warming Is Caused

Key Points:
- Forests play a vital role on Earth.
- Deforestation is a major cause of global warming.
-
-
-

?

WORD ORIGIN

hectare
nutrients
Where are they from?

VISUAL CHALLENGE

In what other ways could you show this information?

... lungs of our planet ...

How Global Warming Is Affecting the Planet

Extreme Weather

Because global warming causes the Earth's atmosphere and oceans to become warmer, more water evaporates into the atmosphere, the atmosphere holds more water and more clouds form. This has had a huge influence on global weather patterns, and the number and intensity of extreme weather events, such as storms, floods, tornadoes and hurricanes, has been increasing.

Countries that usually experience a lot of rain, such as India and Sri Lanka, have been receiving more rain than normal, leading to flooding and landslides. The United States has been experiencing more tornadoes and hurricanes. One of the most devastating was Hurricane Katrina, which destroyed the city of New Orleans in 2005.

In other parts of the world, higher temperatures have been causing more evaporation, less rain and very hot weather. France, Canada and some other countries have experienced searing heat, causing severe forest fires and bushfires. Heat waves have also increased in intensity, and dry areas, such as Australia and parts of Africa, have become even drier.

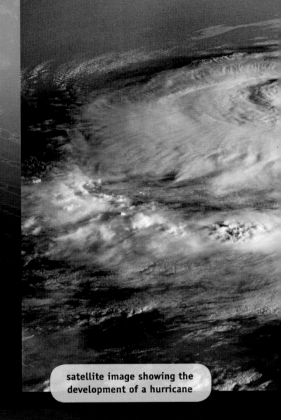

satellite image showing the development of a hurricane

CLARIFY

evaporates
intensity

... flooding,
landslides,
hurricanes,
tornadoes

QUESTION

What do you think are some of the major problems now facing people affected by extreme weather phenomena?

Before ...

After ...

satellite images showing New Orleans before and after Hurricane Katrina

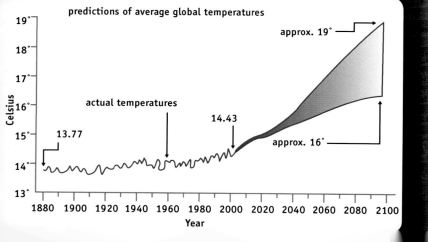

predictions of average global temperatures

approx. 19°

actual temperatures

14.43

13.77

approx. 16°

Celsius

19°
18°
17°
16°
15°
14°
13°

1880 1900 1920 1940 1960 1980 2000 2020 2040 2060 2080 2100

Year

INFERENCE What can you infer about weather patterns and the consequences for people in the future?

boats stranded in what was
once the Aral Sea in central Asia

CLARIFY

drought
erosion
afflicted

... eventually turn into
deserts ...

**QUESTION
GENERATE**

What questions
could you ask?

dust storm blowing across a dry landscape in Arizona, USA

Drought

Abnormally high temperatures and less rainfall than normal for extended periods of time are causing more countries to experience severe drought.

Drought happens when hot, dry weather causes water sources and soil to dry up and plants and trees to wither and die. Forest and grass fires happen more frequently, too, killing plants and trees.

When the plants and trees are gone, the exposed soil absorbs more heat from the sun, pushing temperatures even higher and baking out any moisture left in the soil. Wind erosion can also occur, with dried-out soil blowing over hundreds of kilometres, causing choking, polluting dust storms.

In extreme cases, drought-stricken areas afflicted by wind and sun can eventually turn into deserts.

WORD ORIGIN

drought
desert
Where are they from?

When plants and trees are gone, the exposed soil absorbs more heat.

The Polar Caps and Glaciers

Scientists have recorded the year 2005 as one of the hottest years for more than a century. Rising global temperatures and increased carbon dioxide levels have also been affecting the Earth's coldest places – Greenland and the North and South Poles.

Polar ice is reflective, meaning that 90 per cent of the sun's energy that strikes it is reflected back into space. But, as the bright white ice at the poles melts and shrinks further and further, less heat and light is being reflected back.

Land and ocean waters absorb 90 per cent of the sun's energy, and the more energy is absorbed, the warmer the land and water gets. The result is that each kilometre of ice melts faster than the kilometre before it. Scientists call this the "feedback loop".

Greenland's ice is now melting at a much faster rate than predicted. Its ice caps and glaciers are crumbling, turning to slush and draining away into the ocean.

Icebergs are also melting as they drift in warmer seas and oceans.

1979

satellite images showing the reduction of sea ice around the North Pole in 1979 and 2005

QUESTION

How do you think scientists are able to find out about weather and climate from previous years?

melting Antarctic sea ice breaking up

INFERENCE What can you infer about the effects melting polar caps and glaciers will have on this planet?

Polar bears are drowning because the ice floes they hunt on are melting.

WORD ORIGIN

fauna
flora
habitat

Where are they from?

Warmer water temperatures can kill coral.

CLARIFY

habitat
floes
plankton
krill
sustain

a snowy owl

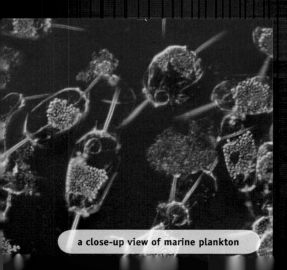

a close-up view of marine plankton

Fauna and Flora

The planet's fauna and flora are being pushed out of their habitats, and even to the brink of extinction, by the many effects of global warming. Warming oceans and higher temperatures at the poles are threatening the future of many animals, including penguins, arctic foxes, snowy owls and polar bears. Many polar bears are drowning as they are forced to swim longer distances between melting ice floes. The bears stalk seals on the ice floes, and the decreasing ice area is also reducing their chances of catching food.

Some species of plankton and krill that prefer colder waters are declining, which is affecting the animals that feed on them, such as birds, whales and other sea creatures.

Coral reefs formed over thousands of years, often referred to as the "rainforests of the sea" because of the thousands of marine species they sustain, are dying in the warmer water temperatures. The warm water causes the coral to expel the algae that nourishes it and gives it its colour. This is called coral bleaching.

OPINION

What is your opinion of global warming now?

17

quiver tree

Global warming is threatening the existence of African elephants, tigers and rhinoceroses. The supply and availability of water and food has a direct influence on the survival rate and breeding patterns of these animals.

Some plant species that live in dry areas, such as the quiver tree in Africa, are moving out of their natural habitats to escape the rising heat and drought.

Tropical rainforests are drying out and forest fires are on the increase, not only destroying the trees but also the many other species of fauna and flora that live among them. The fires have also sent more carbon dioxide floating up into the atmosphere.

QUESTION GENERATE

What questions could you ask?

Animals such as the African elephant could face extinction if global temperatures continue to rise.

Hundreds of animals are lost when forests burn.

SUMMARY CHART

How Global Warming Is Affecting the Planet

Key Points:
- Global warming has had a large influence on global weather patterns.
- The planet's fauna and flora are being pushed out of their habitats.
-
-
-

?

VISUAL CHALLENGE:

In what other ways could you show this information?

中国银行

sickness and death ...

the inside of a human lung
showing symptoms of cancer

a haze of air pollution
hanging over a city

QUESTION

Why do you think
the sick and
elderly are
more affected
by soaring
temperatures?

How Global Warming is Affecting People

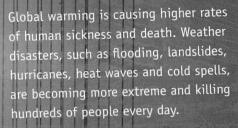

Global warming is causing higher rates of human sickness and death. Weather disasters, such as flooding, landslides, hurricanes, heat waves and cold spells, are becoming more extreme and killing hundreds of people every day.

In cities, rising smog levels are causing higher temperatures and higher rates of heart and lung disease. Some species of pollen-producing plants, such as ragweed, grow faster and produce more pollen when there are higher levels of carbon dioxide. These plants cause allergic reactions in some people. Sometimes they can be severe enough to cause death.

In places where the summer temperatures are usually mild and people are not prepared for extremes, heat waves can be fatal, particularly among the sick and elderly. Soaring temperatures from a heat wave in Europe in 2003 have been linked to around 35,000 deaths across the continent.

the ragweed plant

PREDICT

How else do you think global warming might affect people?

The amount of the Earth's surface now experiencing drought has more than doubled since the 1970s, and millions of people are suffering from malnutrition or dying due to famine and water shortages.

Elsewhere, too much water is killing thousands more. Heavy rains and flooding not only cause drowning, they also affect the quality of water. Old sewer systems can overflow into water supplies, mixing dirty and clean water, causing many water-borne diseases. Stagnant bodies of water in flooded regions make ideal breeding grounds for disease-carrying insects.

Scientists predict that, by the end of the century, global warming will raise ocean levels by 6 metres, due to a combination of melting ice and sea water expanding in warmer temperatures. Large areas of inhabited and cultivated land could be swallowed up in low-lying countries such as Vietnam, India, China and Bangladesh, and some small islands may disappear altogether. Hundreds of thousands of people would become refugees.

WORD ORIGIN

famine
stagnant
Where are they from?

rising ocean levels could swallow up islands like this one

Millions of people do not have enough food or water.

CLARIFY
sewer systems
water-borne
stagnant
refugee

People are being forced out of their homes by rising ocean levels.

INFERENCE

What can you infer from ... hundreds of thousands of people would become refugees ...?

QUESTION GENERATE

What questions could you ask?

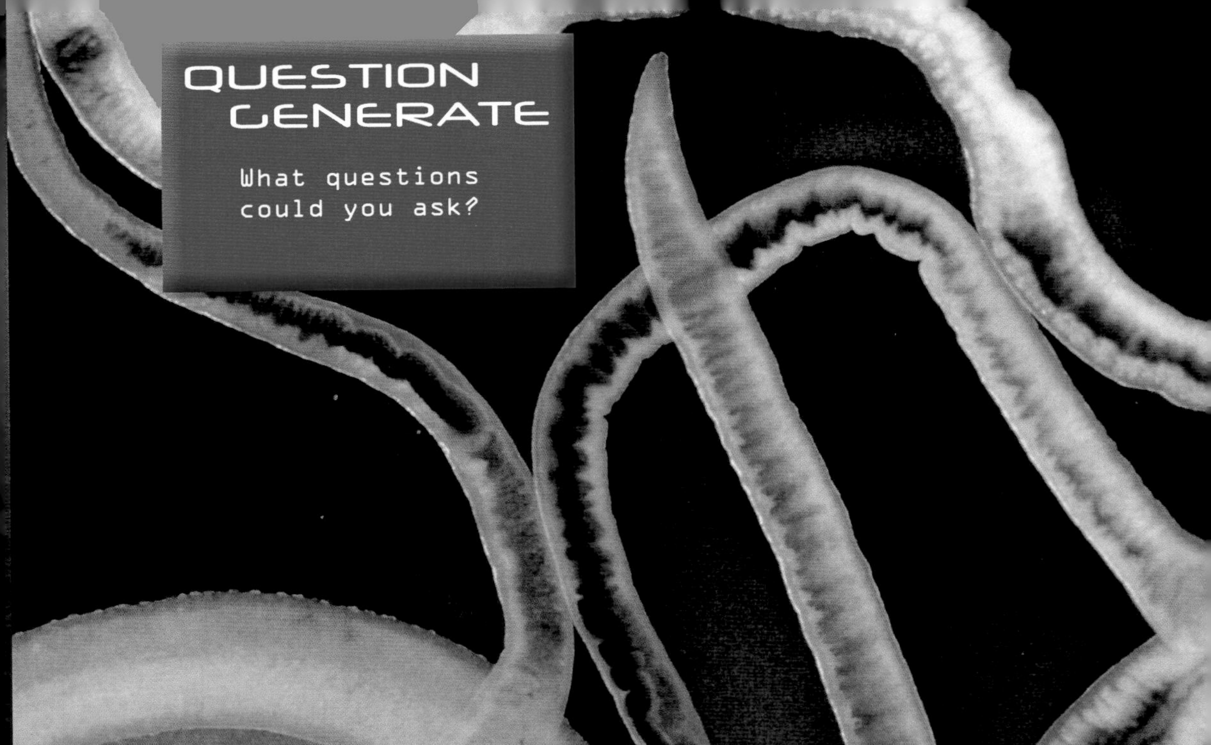

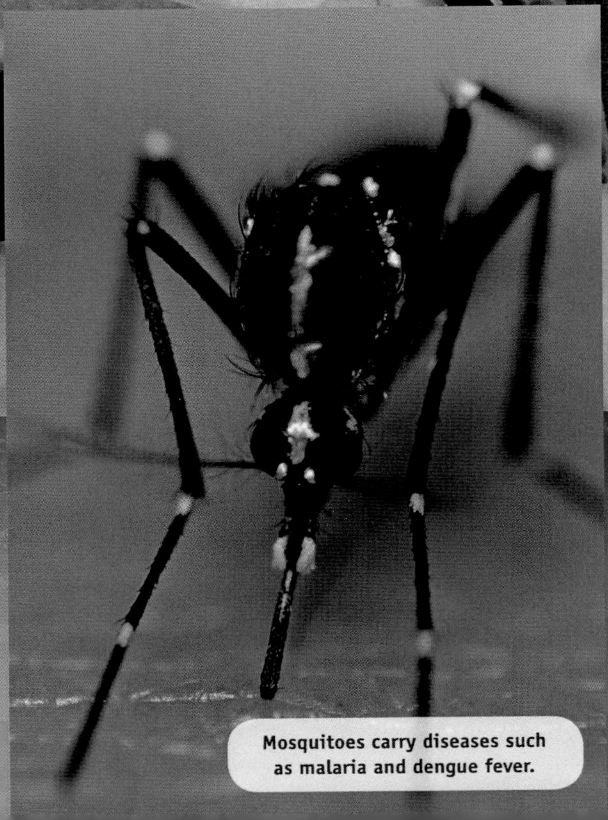

Mosquitoes carry diseases such as malaria and dengue fever.

QUESTION

What do you think is meant by ...

Scientists have discovered a direct relationship between global warming and outbreaks of certain diseases ...?

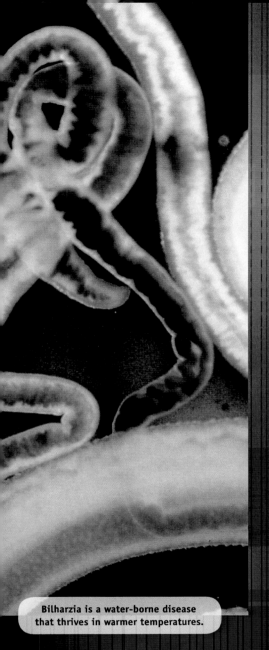

Scientists have discovered a direct relationship between global warming and outbreaks of certain diseases, such as bilharzia and the mosquito-borne diseases of malaria and dengue fever.

Extended periods of hot, damp weather are ideal for mosquitoes to live and breed. Higher temperatures have also increased the number of countries around the world where they can thrive. Malaria now kills more than a million people every year.

Scientists also believe that global warming will cause an increase in the number of diseases carried by food and water. The bacteria and parasites that can contaminate food and drinking water survive best in higher temperatures.

CLARIFY

thrive
contaminate

Bilharzia is a water-borne disease that thrives in warmer temperatures.

... bilharzia,
malaria,
dengue fever ...

Global Warming and the Future

Scientists are not sure if it is too late to reverse some of the changes caused by global warming or whether reductions in emissions of greenhouse gases can still repair the atmosphere. But they do know that, through increased awareness and action, every single person can help and make a difference in many ways.

Choosing energy-efficient appliances, recycling, getting out of the car and walking, cycling or using the bus, and planting trees are just some of the ways that ordinary people can help reduce greenhouse emissions.

Many industries and big businesses have joined the fight against global warming by reducing their emissions of greenhouse gases, and 163 countries have gone one step further by signing the Kyoto Protocol, committing to reduce their greenhouse gases.

By changing the way they treat the planet, humans – the greatest contributors to global warming – alone have the power to save it.

SUMMARY CHART

Earth Alert

Key Points:
-
-
-
-
-

VISUAL CHALLENGE:
In what other ways could you show this information?

Index

Think About the Text

Making connections – what connections can you make to the information presented in **Earth Alert**?

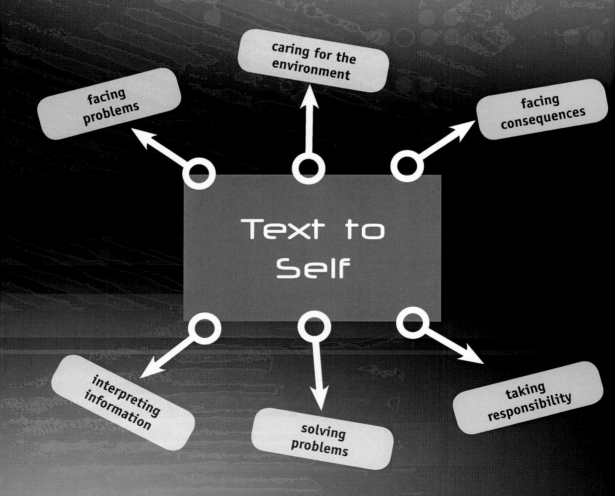

caring for the environment

facing problems

facing consequences

Text to Self

interpreting information

solving problems

taking responsibility

Text to Text

Talk about other informational texts you may have read that have similar features. Compare the texts.

Text to World

Talk about situations in the world that might connect to elements in the text.

Planning an Informational Explanation

1 Select a topic that explains why something is the way it is or how something works.

2 Make a mind map of questions about the topic.

What is global warming?

How is global warming caused?

Earth Alert

How is global warming affecting people?

How is global warming affecting the planet?

3 Locate the information you will need.

Library

Experts

Internet

4   Organise your information using the questions you selected
    as headings.

5   Make a plan.

Introduction:

The impact of humanity on this
planet and its environment is
immense.

Global warming is happening, and
people are to blame.

Points in a coherent and logical sequence:

| How Global Warming | | How Global Warming |
| Is Caused | → | Is Affecting the Planet |

| How Global Warming | | Global Warming and |
| Is Affecting People | → | the Future |

6   Design some visuals to include in your explanation. You can use
    graphs, diagrams, labels, charts, tables, cross-sections . . .

sources of global man-made
carbon dioxide emissions

Writing an Informational Explanation . . .

Have you . . .

- explored causes and effects?

- used scientific and technical vocabulary?

- used the present tense (most explanations are written in the present tense)?

- written in a formal style that is concise and accurate?

- avoided unnecessary descriptive details, metaphors and similes?

- avoided author bias or opinion?

Don't forget . . .

to revisit your writing.
Do you need to change, add or delete
anything to improve your explanation?